THE
Victorian Kitchen
Book of
Candies and Confections

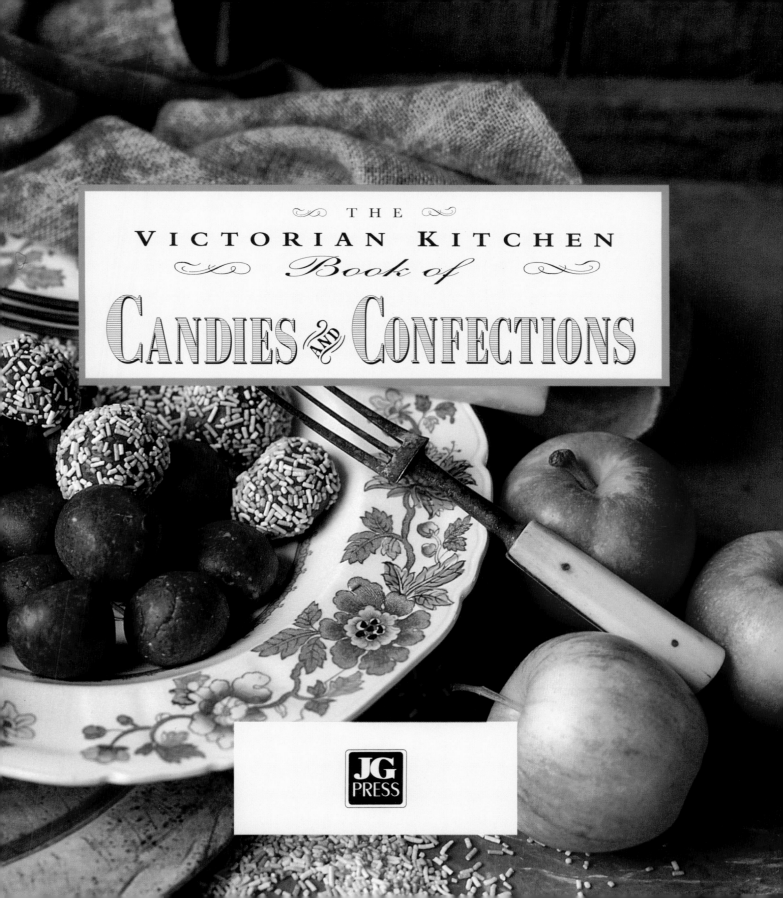

THE VICTORIAN KITCHEN Book of CANDIES AND CONFECTIONS

JG PRESS

The Victorian Kitchen Book Collection

Designed, written and edited by
THE BRIDGEWATER BOOK COMPANY LTD

Text *Amelia Swann*
Art Director *Annie Moss*
Designer *Jane Lanaway*
Managing Editor *Anna Clarkson*
Page make-up *Chris Lanaway*
Photographer *Trevor Wood*
Hand-colored plates *Lorraine Harrison*
Food preparation and styling *Jon Higgins*

Every effort has been made to trace all copyright
holders. The publishers sincerely apologise for
any inadvertant omissions and will be happy to
correct them in any future edition.

CLB 4188

Published in the USA 1995 by JG Press
Distributed by World Publications, Inc.

The JG Press imprint is a trademark of
JG Press, Inc
455 Somerset Avenue
North Dighton, MA 02764

© 1995 CLB Publishing
Godalming, Surrey

Color separation by Sussex Repro, England
Printed and bound in Singapore

ISBN1-57215-051-3

C ONTENTS

INTRODUCTION

By measuring accurately, testing repeatedly, and by taking care to apply the right amount of heat, an amateur should find no difficulty in preparing ... sweetmeats.

MRS. BEETON

CONFECTIONERY was extremely popular with the Victorians – Mrs. Beeton considered "dainty bon-bons" to be part of the dessert – but just as many candies were homemade as were bought.

Many were made with the ingredients at hand in any well-appointed Victorian kitchen – butterscotch and chocolate drops, for example, or fruit and nut laden fudges. It is a treat for the modern cook to rediscover these old

SWEET TIPS

1 **Always use the best sugar and pure, unsalted butter.**
2 **Keep the lid on the saucepan while the sugar is boiling; this will help prevent the sugar from crystallizing.**
3 **Remove any sugar crystals that collect on the sides of the saucepan using a pastry brush dipped in water, otherwise your syrup will go grainy.**
4 **Skim off scum completely as soon as it rises.**
5 **Do not add Cream of Tartar or Tartaric Acid until all the scum has been skimmed off.**
6 **When cooking with molasses or brown sugar, use a large pan for they boil up very fast and may overflow.**
7 **If you use a sugar thermometer, keep it in a jar of warm water in between testings; this will keep it clean and prevent damage if it gets too cold.**

I am glad that my Adonis hath a sweet tooth in his head.

JOHN LYLY

recipes. Making candies at home means that you can be sure that the ingredients are wholesome, and control the kinds of additives used; it can also be great fun for the children in the family to learn how to cook by making traditional old-fashioned candies such as lemon drops, taffy, and barley sugar.

The recipes in this book are a mere sweet and sticky handful of the many kinds of candies and confections made at home in the Victorian kitchen. The recipes are based on authentic sources adapted for modern kitchens.

Most candy recipes REQUIRE YOU TO BOIL THE SUGAR SYRUP TO A CERTAIN PRECISE HEAT. THIS IS EASY TO MEASURE ACCURATELY IF YOU HAVE A SUGAR THERMOMETER, BUT THERE ARE SIMPLE, PRACTICAL TESTS YOU CAN USE TO CHECK THAT THE SYRUP IS READY.

Soft or Small Ball Stage

Drop a small amount of the sugar into a glass of cold water. If it can be formed into a small, soft, malleable bulb, you have reached the soft or small ball stage (240°F).

Hard or Large Ball Stage

After the soft ball stage has been passed, boil the sugar a bit longer then drop a small amount of the sugar into a glass of cold water. If it forms a large, hard ball you have reached the hard ball stage (from 250°F to 290°F, depending on recipe.)

Soft or Small Crack Stage

Carry on boiling, then drop a small amount of the sugar into a glass of cold water. If it can be snapped audibly but sticks to the teeth when bitten, you have reached the soft or small crack stage (290°F).

Hard or Large Crack Stage

Boil further after the soft crack stage, then drop a small amount of sugar into a glass of cold water. If it crackles, snaps with a loud crack when pressed and does not stick to the teeth when bitten, you have reached the hard or large crack stage (300°F).

A CORNUCOPIA OF CONFECTIONERY
FROM THE VICTORIAN KITCHEN

CHOCOLATE AND NUT FUDGE

This dark, delicious fudge would make an ideal indulgent present packed in a pretty container.

INGREDIENTS

3½ cups Granulated Sugar
1¼ cups Fresh Milk
8oz Plain Chocolate
2 T. Butter
Pinch of Salt
Pinch of Cream of Tartar
½ cup Chopped Mixed Nuts
1t. Coffee Essence
1t. Vanilla Essence

METHOD

❧ In a large saucepan gently heat together the sugar, milk, chocolate, butter, salt, and cream of tartar until smooth. Increase the heat and boil until the temperature reaches 240°F. Use a sugar thermometer to measure this accurately.

❧ Remove the pan from the heat and allow the mixture to cool a little before adding the chopped nuts and the coffee and vanilla essence. Beat the mixture well as it cools; it will become thicker and progressively more difficult to work with a spoon.

❧ Pour the fudge onto a lightly greased cookie sheet and allow to cool. Cut into chunks using a hot knife.

Sweets to the Sweet

To send fudge or toffee by mail, line buttered tins with wax paper and pour in the candy mixture while it is still hot. Allow to cool, then mark into squares. When it is completely cold, cover with a layer of wax paper, put the lid on, and wrap appropriately.

COOK'S TIP

Mix in 1 T. candied fruit with the chopped nuts to make Fruity Chocolate and Nut Fudge.

Candied Fruit

If you like it, add a tablespoonful of candied fruit to either of these recipes. Soak the pieces of fruit in boiling water for a few minutes to remove the sugar and soften them so that they will be easier to cut. Angelica is particularly good with these fudges.

CARAMEL FUDGE

This gorgeous creamy fudge, based on an authentic American recipe of the period is dangerously easy to make.

INGREDIENTS

$3\frac{1}{2}$ cups Granulated Sugar
$\frac{1}{4}$ cups Cold Water
$1\frac{1}{4}$ cups Fresh Milk
Few Drops of Vanilla Essence

METHOD

❦ Place 1 cup of the sugar in a saucepan with the cold water and place over a gentle heat until the sugar has dissolved. Turn the heat up and allow the liquid to come to a boil. Continue boiling until the temperature on the sugar thermometer reads 320°F, then remove the pan from the heat: the sugar should be a beautiful golden brown color.

❦ Place the remaining sugar in a saucepan with the milk and gently bring to a boil Add the caramelized sugar to the pan. Continue boiling the mixture until the sugar thermometer reads 240°F, taking care to stir the mixture regularly to prevent it from burning.

❦ Remove the pan from the heat and beat the mixture until it becomes thick and creamy. Pour the fudge into buttered pans and allow to cool completely before cutting into chunks.

COFFEE FUDGE

This is a sophisticated kind of fudge that will be much appreciated when served after dinner with coffee. The recipe is based on an authentic American one of the period.

INGREDIENTS

2¼ cups Granualted Sugar
1¼ cups Strong Coffee
1 T. Butter
½ cup Chopped Walnuts
Few Drops of Almond Essence

METHOD

❧ Place the sugar, coffee, and butter in a saucepan and place on a gentle heat until the sugar and butter have dissolved.

❧ Increase the heat and bring the pan to a boil, stir constantly until the sugar thermometer reads 240°F, then remove the pan from the heat. Stir in the chopped walnuts and almond essence and beat the cooling mixture until it thickens.

❧ Pour the fudge onto a buttered cookie sheet and allow to cool completely before cutting into portions.

> Complacencies
> of the peignoir, and late
> Coffee and oranges in a sunny chair.
>
> WALLACE STEVENS,
> SUNDAY MORNING

COFFEE FUDGE, AN AFTER-DINNER SWEET TREAT

FIG AND RAISIN FUDGE

This wholesome, sustaining fudge, stuffed with stamina-giving fruit, is just what you need to accompany you on a bracing walk in the country.

INGREDIENTS

3½ cups Granulated Sugar
1¼ cups Fresh Milk
½ cup Dried Figs, Chopped
1 cup Raisins
½ cup Chopped Walnuts
1 T. Butter

METHOD

❦ Place the sugar and milk in a saucepan and gently heat until the sugar has completely dissolved. Increase the heat and bring the liquid to a boil, continue boiling until the sugar solution reaches 240°F. If you do not have a sugar thermometer to hand this can be checked by dropping a small amount of the solution into cold water; if a soft ball forms the correct temperature has been reached.

❦ Remove the pan from the heat and beat in the remaining ingredients. As the mixture cools, the fudge will become thicker and more difficult to beat.

❦ Spread the fudge over a buttered cookie sheet. Allow to cool completely before cutting into squares.

Walking for walking's sake may be as highly laudable as it is held to be by those who practise it. My objection to it is that it stops the brain.
MAX BEERBOHM

WHOLESOME AND HEALTHY, FIG AND RAISIN FUDGE

RASPBERRY NUT FUDGE

FUDGE WITH WHIPPED CREAM

This elegant, creamy confection of chocolate, cream, and vanilla is made for afternoon indulgence. It is based on an authentic American recipe of the period.

INGREDIENTS

3 ½ cups Soft Brown Sugar
1 ¼ cups Milk
Pinch of Salt
4 oz Plain Chocolate
½ cup Butter
1 ¼ cups Heavy Cream, Whipped
Few Drops of Vanilla essence
½ cup Chopped Walnuts

METHOD

❧ Place the sugar, milk, salt, chocolate, and butter in a saucepan and place on a low heat, stirring continuously until the solids have melted to leave a smooth mixture.

❧ Turn the heat up and bring the mixture to a boil. Continue heating until the sugar thermometer registers 250°F or until the mixture forms hard balls when small amounts are dropped into cold water.

❧ Remove the saucepan from the heat and beat for several minutes then add the whipped cream, vanilla essence, and chopped walnuts. Continue to beat the mixture until it has cooled and become stiff.

❧ Pour the fudge into well-greased pans and allow to cool completely before cutting into pieces.

RASPBERRY NUT FUDGE

Simple and homey, yet delicious, this fudge can be made with store-cupboard ingredients. It's easy for older children to prepare, as long as they have adult help when boiling the syrup.

COOK'S TIP

Substitute the pecans with walnuts if you prefer; you can also make this fudge with strawberry jam and almonds.

INGREDIENTS

2 ¼ cups Granulated Sugar
Pinch of Cream of Tartar
5 T. Homemade Raspberry Jam
1 ¼ cups Fresh Water
½ cup Chopped Pecans

METHOD

❧ Place the sugar and cream of tartar in a saucepan and pour in the water. Place the pan over a gentle heat until the sugar has dissolved, then increase the heat and bring the liquid to a boil. Continue boiling the sugar solution, stirring continually, until the sugar thermometer registers 250°F. Pour the sugar solution into a wet bowl and allow it to stand for a few minutes.

❧ Warm the raspberry jam in a saucepan with a little cold water and pass it through a sieve to remove the seeds. Stir the warmed jam into the sugar solution and beat together until the mixture thickens and begins to go grainy.

❧ Stir in the chopped pecans and spread the fudge into a buttered pan. Cut into chunks when the fudge has cooled completely.

Mr. Burchell ... at the conclusion of every sentence would cry out fudge! – an expression which displeased us all.

OLIVER GOLDSMITH,
THE VICAR OF WAKEFIELD

ELEGANCE AND INDULGENCE
COMBINE IN FUDGE WITH WHIPPED CREAM

DUBLIN ROCK AND EDINBURGH ROCK,
THE CANDIES OF GAELIC INSPIRATION

DUBLIN ROCK

This candy was very popular in the Dublin of the 1890s. It's a very rich candy, reminiscent of marzipan. It was the custom to break it up into rough, jagged "rocks" and serve garnished with slivers of angelica to look like weeds or lichen peeping through the boulders.

INGREDIENTS

½ cup Unsalted Butter
2 cups Ground Almonds
4 T. Granulated Sugar
1 T Brandy

METHOD

❧ Melt the butter over a low heat and pour it into a bowl. Add the ground almonds, sugar, and brandy and continue beating until the mixture has cooled and begun to set.

❧ Leave overnight until set solid then break into lumps. The rock should have a soft texture but be quite firm.

A Candy Hook

If you make lots of candies at home, a candy hook is very useful. It is easier to pull candy over a hook than just with your hands, and it makes the candy lighter and fluffier. Mrs. Beeton recommends that a strong iron hook "should be fixed firmly on a wall about 5 feet from the floor, according to the height of the worker."

In Dublin's Fair City
Where the girls are so pretty
I first set my eyes on
Sweet Molly Malone.
ANON

Sweet spring, full of sweet days and roses
A box wherein sweets compacted lie.
GEORGE HERBERT

EDINBURGH ROCK

Edinburgh Rock, a specialty of Scotland's capital, was popular with the Victorians. It looks complicated to make, but is well worth the effort.

INGREDIENTS

2 cups Granulated Sugar
1 cup Water
Pinch of Cream Of Tartar
Few Drops of Lemon Flavoring

METHOD

❧ Place the sugar and water in a saucepan and place over a low heat, stirring all the time until the sugar has dissolved. Add the cream of tartar and increase the heat to bring the syrup to a boil. Continue boiling until the temperature reaches 280°F by the sugar thermometer or forms a hard ball when a small amount is dropped into cold water.

❧ Remove the pan from the heat, stir in the lemon flavoring and allow to cool for a couple of minutes.

❧ Pour the thick syrup onto a greased marble slab and work with a buttered palette knife folding the edges into the middle. This keeps the mixture pliable and easy to work with.

❧ When cool enough to handle, rub a little oil on the fingers and pull the mixture between outstretched arms. Immediately fold the mixture in half and repeat the process until the mixture looses its shine.

❧ Cut the candy into strips and lay them out on wax paper for a couple of days to dry completely before transferring them to an airtight containers to store.

The red rose whispers of passion,
And the white rose breathes of love;
O, the red rose is a falcon,
And the white rose is a dove.

But I send you a cream-white rosebud
With a flush on its petal tips;
For the love that is present and sweetest
Has a kiss of desire on the lips.

JOHN BOYLE O'REILLY

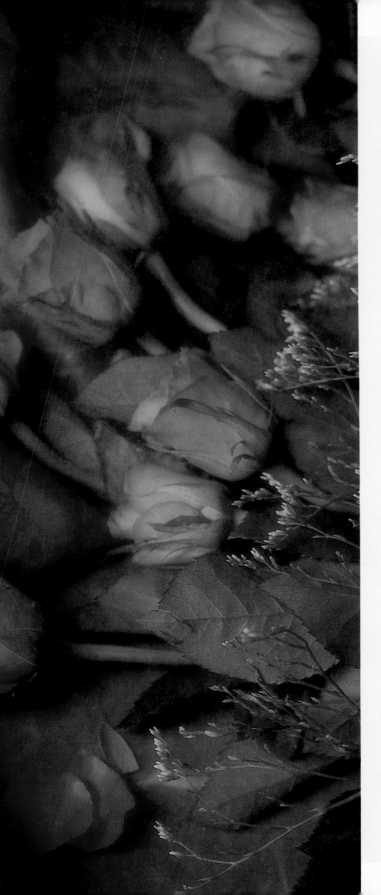

Rose Tablet

Palest pink, honey sweet, Rose Tablet is the confection for young Victorian maidens, blushing under the adoring regard of their many admirers. Serve it on a bed of rose petals.

INGREDIENTS

1 T. Glucose
4½ cups Granulated Sugar
1¼ cups Fresh Water
Pinch of Cream of Tartar
2t. Rose Extract
Few Drops of Red Coloring

METHOD

❦ Put the sugar, glucose, and water in a saucepan and place over a low heat until the sugar has dissolved, stirring all the time. Increase the heat and bring the syrup to a boil, add the cream of tartar to the pan and stop stirring.

❦ When the syrup reaches 240°F by the sugar thermometer, or forms a soft ball when small amounts of syrup are dropped into cold water, remove the pan from the heat and allow to cool for a couple of minutes.

❦ Add the rose extract and coloring and stir the mixture until it becomes thick. Pour into a well-buttered pan. When completely cooled the mixture will have set and you will be able to cut it into portions.

Almond Tablet is made with milk instead of water, and vanilla and almonds instead of rose extract and coloring.

Brazil Nut Caramels

This chunky, chewy taffy is ideal for wintry feasts such as Halloween, Thanksgiving, or Christmas.

INGREDIENTS

2¹/₂ cups Heavy Cream
2¹/₄ cups Granulated Sugar
2 T. Glucose
4 T. Butter
Few Drops of Vanilla Essence
¹/₂ cup Chopped Brazil Nuts

METHOD

❧ Place 1 cup of cream and the sugar in a saucepan and heat gently until the sugar has completely dissolved. Add the glucose to the pan and increase the heat to bring the mixture to a boil. Continue boiling until the temperature reaches 240°F by the sugar thermometer or to the soft ball stage when tested in cold water.

❧ Add the remaining cream and butter and continue boiling until the sugar thermometer registers 250°F or to the hard ball stage when tested in cold water.

❧ Remove the pan from the heat and stir in the vanilla essence and chopped brazil nuts and pour the mixture onto a well-greased cookie sheet. Leave to cool and mark out the portions with a sharp knife.

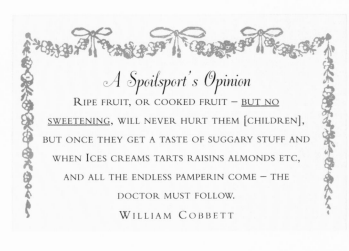

A Spoilsport's Opinion

RIPE FRUIT, OR COOKED FRUIT – <u>BUT NO SWEETENING</u>, WILL NEVER HURT THEM [CHILDREN], BUT ONCE THEY GET A TASTE OF SUGGARY STUFF AND WHEN ICES CREAMS TARTS RAISINS ALMONDS ETC, AND ALL THE ENDLESS PAMPERIN COME – THE DOCTOR MUST FOLLOW.

WILLIAM COBBETT

I'm Charlie's Aunt from Brazil, where the nuts come from.
BRANDON THOMAS

CREAM CARAMELS

Rich, creamy and everybody's favorite, these cream caramels are based on an authentic American recipe of the period. They are very easy to make, and disappear very quickly.

INGREDIENTS

2¼ cups Granulated Sugar
⅔ cup Water
⅔ cup Heavy Cream
½ cup Glucose
2 T. Butter

METHOD

❧ Put the sugar and water in a saucepan and place over a low heat until the sugar has dissolved. Increase the heat and bring the solution to a boil. Add the glucose and continue boiling until the temperature reaches 240°F by the sugar thermometer or forms a soft ball when a small amount is dropped into cold water.

❧ Add the cream and butter and continue boiling, stirring all the time, until the sugar thermometer reads 250°F or the hard ball stage has been reached.

❧ Remove the pan from the heat and pour the caramel into buttered pans and allow to cool. When cold cut the caramel into squares and wrap the individual candies in wax paper.

We do not know of an article so generally a favorite with all classes as caramel.
PHILADELPHIA TIMES,
SEPTEMBER 4TH, 1884

CHOCOLATE CARAMELS

These creamy caramels are based on a recipe from Mrs. Beeton. You could make them to pack into a small hamper of delights for chocolate loving friends, together with Chocolate and Nut Fudge (see page 8).

INGREDIENTS

2¼ cups Granulated Sugar
1¼ cups Milk
1¼ cups Heavy Cream
1t. Vanilla Essence
3oz Dark Chocolate, Grated

METHOD

❧ Place the sugar and milk in a saucepan and gently warm over a low heat until the sugar has completely dissolved. Add the cream to the pan and increase the heat so the liquid comes to a boil.

❧ Dissolve the chocolate in a small amount of boiling water and add it to the pan. Continue boiling until the temperature reaches 250°F by the sugar thermometer or the hard ball stage when tested in cold water.

❧ Remove the pan from the heat and pour the caramel into buttered pans and allow to cool. When cold cut into pieces using a buttered knife.

WALNUT CREAMS, SOPHISTICATED NUTTY TREATS

WALNUT CREAMS

These sophisticated candies are simple to make as they involve no cooking. You could flavor the cream mixture with cinnamon or strong coffee, or replace the walnuts with almonds. A selection of different flavored creams would make an elegant contribution to a formal dessert.

INGREDIENTS

2 cups Confectionery Sugar

1 Egg White

1t. Rose Extract

1 cup Walnut Halves

Egg White and Shredded Coconut for Decoration

METHOD

❧ Sieve the confectionery sugar into a mixing bowl, add the egg white and rose extract and beat together until smooth.

❧ Spread some confectionery sugar over a work surface and turn the paste out. Knead gently for a few minutes. Break off small amounts of the mixture and form into ball shapes using the palms of your hands, then sandwich them between two halves of walnut.

❧ Clean away any surplus cream and brush the edges with a little egg white before rolling them in the shredded coconut.

COOK'S TIP

For a real touch of luxury, omit the coconut and dip the sandwiched walnuts into melted chocolate.

Deep violets, you liken to
The kindest eyes that lock on you
Without a thought disloyal.

ELIZABETH BARRETT BROWNING

CREAMED VIOLETS

These very elegant, refined candies look beautiful arranged on a pretty glass dish or, if you are fortunate, an antique bonbonnière.

INGREDIENTS

$2\frac{1}{4}$ cups Granulated Sugar

$1\frac{1}{4}$ cups Heavy Cream

Pinch of Cream of Tartar

4 T. Clear Honey

1 Egg White, Stiffly Beaten

Few Drops of Violet Food Coloring

Few Drops of Vanilla Essence

COOK'S TIP

Decorate with crystallized violet if desired; arrange pieces of violet on the candies before they have dried completely.

METHOD

❧ Gently heat the sugar and cream until the sugar has dissolved. Add the cream of tartar and honey and increase the heat to bring the syrup to a boil, stirring constantly. Continue boiling until the temperature of the syrup reaches 240°F on a sugar thermometer or forms soft balls when small amounts are dropped into cold water.

❧ Remove the pan from the heat and stir in the beaten egg white, food coloring and vanilla essence and beat until the mixture is thick and creamy.

❧ Drop small amounts of the mixture onto wax paper and using a sharp stick shape each one into violet petals. Leave until the violets have dried completely.

Crystallized Leaves and Flowers.

To crystallize leaves from violets, roses, lilac, borage, or other pretty flowers, first remove the stems, wash the blooms, and leave them on clean paper to dry. Make a sugar syrup using 5 cups sugar to every 2 cups water and a pinch of cream of tartar. Boil until it reaches 240°F, or a drop of the mixture forms a soft ball in cold water. Remove from the heat, add the flowers to the syrup, making sure they are well covered. Boil up then pour onto a cold dish. Leave for 24 hours, strain the syrup off, reboil it, and add the flowers again. Remove from the heat, stir until the syrup goes grainy, then pour out onto sheets of wax paper. When dry, pick the flowers out from the sugar.

LEMON CREAMS, DAINTY BON-BONS FOR DESSERT

ORANGE CREAMS

Make equally luscious
Orange Creams using
orange juice, orange
flavoring, and candied
orange peel.

COOK'S TIP

Dip candied peel
into hot water for a
few seconds to make
it pliable enough
to use for
decoration.

LEMON CREAMS

*These tangy Lemon Creams melt in the mouth. They look
gratifyingly professional when made up, certainly good enough to
give as a present or to serve at a special occasion.*

INGREDIENTS

*2 cups Confectionery Sugar
Pinch of Cream Of Tartar
Lemon Juice
Yellow Coloring
Lemon Flavoring
Yellow Coloring
Candied Lemon Peel for Decoration
Milk
Confectionery Sugar*

METHOD

❧ Sieve the confectionery sugar and cream of tartar into a large
mixing bowl. Slowly add sufficient lemon juice to form a stiff paste and
add a few drops of coloring to turn the candy mixture a pale yellow.

❧ Dust a marble slab or work surface with confectionery sugar and
knead the mixture for a few minutes, incorporating a few drops of
lemon flavoring. Use more confectionery sugar to dust a rolling pin
and roll out the paste to approximately ¼in thick and cut out small
candies using fancy cutters.

❧ Reroll the trimmings and cut out more candiess until all the paste
has been used. Decorate with a small piece of candied peel or a
crystallized flower leaf pressed into the center of each candy.

Opera Creams

Re-create opera nights with Gilbert & Sullivan at the Savoy or Puccini at Covent Garden; invite your friends (or indulge yourself) with a dish of these elegant, sophisticated candies, coffee and brandy, and your favorite tenor on disk.

I think an Opera box a very substantial comfort.

THOMAS LOVE PEACOCK, CROTCHET CASTLE

INGREDIENTS

3½ cups Granulated Sugar
1¼ cups Heavy Cream
⅔ cup Fresh Milk
1 T. Glucose
2 cups Confectionery Sugar
1t. Ginger Flavoring
1t. Coffee Flavoring
Few Drops of Brown Food Coloring

METHOD

❧ Put the sugar, cream, milk, and glucose into a saucepan and place over a gentle heat until the sugar has completely dissolved. Increase the heat and bring the mixture to a boil. Continue boiling until the temperature reaches 240°F on the sugar thermometer or the soft ball stage when tested in cold water.

❧ Remove the boiling syrup from the heat and allow to stand for a minute, then pour it into a wet bowl and allow to continue cooling. After a few minutes, begin beating the mixture with a wooden spoon and when it has become thicker, leave to stand for an hour.

❧ Divide the cooled mixture into two and knead the ginger flavoring into one half and the coffee flavoring and food coloring into the other. Use some of the confectionery sugar to soak up any excess moisture while kneading the paste.

❧ Place the flavored paste in separate bowls and leave covered for three hours, then roll out each paste and cut into small squares. Lay the finished candies on wax paper and allow to dry in the open air for 24 hours.

OPERA CREAMS AND PEPPERMINT CREAMS, SUITABLE CONFECTIONS FOR HIGH SOCIETY

PEPPERMINT CREAMS

❧

These delicious creams are easy to make since no cooking is involved. Rolled thin, they make ideal after-dinner mints.

INGREDIENTS

1 Egg White
Peppermint Flavoring
Confectionery Sugar
Melted Dark Chocolate For
Decoration (Optional)

❧

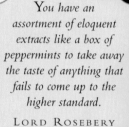

You have an assortment of eloquent extracts like a box of peppermints to take away the taste of anything that fails to come up to the higher standard.

LORD ROSEBERY

METHOD

❧ Place the egg white in a mixing bowl and add a few drops of peppermint flavoring. Stir in sieved confectionery sugar until the mixture becomes quite firm and dry and can be easily manipulated.

❧ Take small amounts of the mixture and form into balls between the palms of your hands. Place the balls on a sheet of wax paper and apply light pressure to each one with a palette knife to flatten it a little.

❧ Leave the creams in a cool place to dry. When completely dry, brush each cream with a little melted dark chocolate if desired.

COOK'S TIP

If you prefer, roll out the peppermint paste with a rolling pin dusted with confectionery sugar and use cutters to make small round candies.

BURNT ALMONDS

These delicious, elegant candies are based on instructions given by Mrs. Hislop, cook to Lady Shaftesbury, who pronounced them "very good." Serve them with coffee or as part of dessert, along with irresistible Chocolate Almonds (see below).

INGREDIENTS

1½ cups Blanched Almonds
2¼ cups Granulated Sugar
1¼ cups Water
Pinch of Cream of Tartar
Few Drops of Almond Essence
2t. Gum Arabic

METHOD

❦ Spread the almonds over a cookie sheet and place in a moderate oven until they brown lightly. Check them constantly because they can quickly burn. When sufficiently colored, remove them from the oven, place them in a saucepan and heat very gently.

❦ In a separate saucepan, bring the sugar, water, and cream of tartar to a boil and continue heating until the temperature registers 290°F on a sugar thermometer.

❦ Take the syrup from the heat and add it to the pan of almonds a little at a time, tossing them to coat them evenly, until all the syrup has been used. A few drops of almond essence can be added at this stage. Tip the coated almonds from the saucepan and allow 24 hours to dry.

❦ To glaze the almonds, place the gum arabic in a saucepan and heat gently, add the almonds to the pan and toss until well glazed. Leave them in a warm place to dry. Store the finished almonds in airtight jars.

CHOCOLATE ALMONDS

Blanch as many almonds as you like and lay them on a cookie sheet in a low oven until they are slightly brown. Melt some of your favorite chocolate and dip the almonds in it when they are cold. Leave to harden.

WHIZZ BURNT ALMONDS *in a food processor, to make praline powder for flavoring cakes or ice creams.*

If a little child came in to ask for an ounce of almond confits, she always added one more by way of a "make weight."
MRS. GASKELL,
CRANFORD

PRESERVED PLUMS

These are sugar plums, a great favorite in the 18th century that lasted well into the Victorian era. Served as dessert with Burnt Almonds, they make a very elegant dish. This is based on a recipe from Mrs. Beeton.

INGREDIENTS

2lb Just Ripe Plums
1¼ cups Cold Water
4½ cups Granulated Sugar
1¼ cups Fresh Water

METHOD

❦ Wash the plums and prick them well all over with a needle. Place them in a saucepan, cover with cold water and place on the heat. When the water begins to boil remove the pan from the heat and drain the water from the fruit.

❦ Heat together the sugar and water until the sugar dissolves, then place the syrup and the plums together in a saucepan and bring the pan to a boil and allow to boil gently for 15 to 20 minutes. Skim the surface to remove any scum that may rise and remove the pan from the heat. Allow the plums to steep in the cooling syrup overnight.

❦ The following day carefully transfer the fruit and syrup to a wide-necked jar and leave in a warm place for 48 hours.

❦ Drain the syrup from the plums and place the fruit on cookie sheets. Sprinkle over a little confectionery sugar and place in a cool oven, 250°F, until the fruit has dried. Store the preserved fruit in a very dry place.

COOK'S TIP

If the plums begin to shrivel in the syrup, it means they are not absorbing the liquid; prick them over again without removing them from the pan.

Compliments flew about like sugar plums at an Italian carnival.

SIR WALTER SCOTT

PRESERVED PLUMS FOR A
SPECIAL CHRISTMAS TREAT.

NOGAT

Nougat, sticky, nut crammed and rather exotic, is a French notion; Eliza Acton, who had lived in France, gave a very detailed recipe for it. This one, which is rather simpler, is based on Mrs. Beeton's version.

INGREDIENTS

1 cup Confectionery Sugar
5 T. Honey
2 Egg Whites
1 cup Blanched Almonds
Handful of Pistachios or Chopped Mixed Nuts

METHOD

❦ Place the confectionery sugar, honey, and egg whites in a saucepan and cook over a low heat, stirring continually, until the mixture thickens and turns white. A simple test to check that it has cooked sufficiently is to drop a small amount of the mixture into cold water; if it immediately hardens, remove the saucepan from the heat and stir in the blanched almonds and the pistachios or mixed nuts.

❦ Turn the nougat out onto a work surface covered with confectionery sugar and form it into a ball shape. Line a small pan with wax paper and press the nougat into it, making sure it spreads into all four corners. Cover with more wax and place some weight on it until completely cold.

❦ Cut the cold nougat into squares and store in a dry container until required.

COOK'S TIP

Vary your nougat by adding your favorite flavorings: rose, orange, lemon, vanilla, peppermint, and your favorite kinds of nuts along with the essential almonds.

NOUGAT, THE SUMMERY FLAVOR OF FRENCH SUNSHINE

THE PORTION *of almonds can be diminished at pleasure, but the nougat should always be well filled with them.*

ELIZA ACTON

That learned and exquisite mixture now designated under the name of Nougat.

ALEXIS SOYER

TURKISH DELIGHT FOR A TASTE OF EXOTICA

TURKISH DELIGHT

The Victorians delighted in things eastern and exotic; Edward Fitzgerald's translation of the
Persian poems of Omar Khayyam was a runaway bestseller. Imagine reading those haunting,
languid lyrics while eating melting mouthfuls of this delicate, rose-scented confection.

'Tis never too
late for delight,
my dear.

THOMAS
MOORE,
THE YOUNG
MAY MOON.

INGREDIENTS

4½ cups Granulated Sugar

5 cups Cold Water

½ cup Cornstarch

3 cups Confectionery Sugar

4 T. Clear Honey

1t. Lemon Flavoring

1t. Rose Flavoring

½t. Tartaric Acid

Few Drops of Green Food Coloring

METHOD

❧ Set the granulated sugar and 2 cups of the water to boil in a
saucepan. Once boiling, heat the mixture until the temperature reaches
240°F on the sugar thermometer, or until small amounts of the syrup
dropped into cold water form soft balls.

❧ While the syrup is boiling, make a paste using the cornstarch and
1 cup of the water. Boil the remaining water and add to the cornstarch
paste along with the confectionery sugar.

❧ Heat the cornstarch mixture over a low heat until it thickens, then
slowly add the boiling syrup, stirring continuously until it is all
incorporated. Add the remaining ingredients, stir, and pour the
mixture into buttered pans. When cold, cut the Turkish Delight
into squares and dust liberally with confectionery sugar.

WALNUT TAFFY

This taffy, crammed with walnuts, a Victorian favorite, sets to a very attractive clear amber.

INGREDIENTS

½ cup Chopped Walnuts
3½ cups Granulated Sugar
1¼ cups Water
Good Pinch of Salt
2 Drops of Acetic Acid
1t. Lemon Flavoring

From whence, it being only a step to the toffy shop, what could be more simple than to go there and fill their pockets.

THOMAS HUGHES,
TOM BROWN'S SCHOOLDAYS

METHOD

❧ Sprinkle the chopped walnuts over a greased cookie sheet and put to one side.

❧ Put the sugar and water in a saucepan and place over a low heat until the sugar has completely dissolved. Using a pastry brush, wipe around the sides of the saucepan to collect any crystals that may have formed. Increase the heat and bring the syrup to a boil. Continue boiling until the temperature reaches 300°F by the sugar thermometer or forms hard, brittle threads when plunged into cold water.

❧ Remove the pan from the heat and add the salt, acetic acid, and lemon flavoring and pour over the chopped walnuts. Allow to cool completely before breaking into chunks.

A TRIO OF TASTY TAFFY: ALMOND, MOLASSES, AND WALNUT

Molasses Taffy

Rich, dark and sticky, molasses taffy, was a Victorian favorite.
This is based on a recipe from Mrs. Beeton.

INGREDIENTS

4 T. Brown Sugar
3–4 T. Vinegar
2½ cups Molasses
½ t. Baking Soda
2 T. Butter
Few Drops Of Almond Essence

METHOD

❧ Place the brown sugar and vinegar in a saucepan and heat gently until the sugar has dissolved completely. Add the molasses and increase the heat to bring the pan to a boil. Once boiling, measure the temperature using a sugar thermometer and when it reaches 240°F, remove the pan from the heat.

❧ Add the baking soda dissolved in a small amount of hot water, the butter and a few drops of almond essence and return the pan to the heat. Continue boiling until the sugar thermometer reads 290°F.

❧ Remove the pan from the heat and pour the taffy into a well-greased pan. When lightly set, mark the taffy into sections using a sharp knife. Allow to cool completely before breaking into pieces.

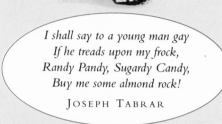

*I shall say to a young man gay
If he treads upon my frock,
Randy Pandy, Sugardy Candy,
Buy me some almond rock!*

JOSEPH TABRAR

ALMOND TAFFY

This is delicious, subtle tasting taffy, suitable for grown-ups as well as children. It is based on Mrs. Beeton's recipe.

INGREDIENTS

2¼ cups Granulated Sugar
1¼ cups Water
Pinch of Cream of Tartar
1 cup Whole Almonds, Blanched
Few Drops of Almond Essence

METHOD

❧ Put the sugar and water in a saucepan and place on a low heat until the sugar has completely dissolved. Add the cream of tartar and increase the heat to bring the mixture to a boil. Continue heating until the syrup reaches 240°F. This can be measured accurately using a sugar thermometer.

❧ Once the temperature has been reached, remove the pan from the heat and stir in the blanched almonds – these are best split in half with a sharp knife – and the almond essence. Return the pan to the heat and reboil to a temperature of 290°F.

❧ Pour the liquid taffy into greased pans and allow to cool. When set but still warm, mark out the portions with a sharp knife and leave to go completely cold before cutting.

*Half a pound of twopenny rice,
Half a pound of treacle,
That's the way the money goes,
Pop! goes the weasel.*

ANON

DARK, SWEET, AND CREAMY RUSSIAN TAFFY

RUSSIAN TAFFY

Let it be understood that a Russian is a delightful person till he tucks in his shirt.

RUDYARD KIPLING

There are many versions of this perennial favorite; it's satisfyingly chewy and substantial, just the thing for winter sleigh rides.

INGREDIENTS

4½ cups Soft Brown Sugar
1 cup Butter
1 T. Water
1¼ cups Heavy Cream
I T. Rose Extract
Few Drops of Vanilla Essence

METHOD

❦ Place the sugar, butter, and water in a saucepan and heat gently until all the ingredients have melted.

❦ Increase the heat and bring the solution to the boil. Add the cream, rose extract, and vanilla essence and stir together.

❦ Continue boiling the mixture until the temperature reaches 250°F on a sugar thermometer, or forms a hard ball when small amounts are dropped into cold water.

❦ Remove the pan from the heat and allow the taffy to go off the boil before pouring into a well-buttered cookie sheet. Leave to cool. Cut the taffy into chunks when partially set.

ÉVERTON TAFFY, A TRADITIONAL TREAT

EVERTON TAFFY

E*verton, now part of Liverpool, has a long history of taffy-making. Everton Taffy, or Toffee, is a venerable confection. Both Eliza Acton and Mrs. Beeton give recipes, but even in the 19th century, Everton boasted an "Ancient Toffee House." This recipe, based on Mrs. Beeton's, gives the authentic taste of a traditional taffy.*

INGREDIENTS

2 1/4 cups Brown Sugar
2/3 cup Water
1/2 cup Butter
Pinch of Cream of Tartar

METHOD

❧ Heat together the sugar and water until the sugar has completely dissolved. Add the cream of tartar to the pan and bring it to a boil, continue boiling until the temperature reaches 240°F on the sugar thermometer or the soft ball stage when dropped in cold water.

❧ Remove the pan from the heat and add the butter cut into small pieces. Continue to boil until the temperature reaches 290°F or soft crack stage. Pour the taffy onto buttered cookie sheets and when cold cut into chunks and wrap individually in wax paper.

TAFFY APPLES

For a really traditional, old-fashioned treat, homemade taffy apples are hard to beat. They are ideal for winter festivities. This is a simple yet authentic recipe that children might like to make themselves, if they have adult help when cooking the syrup.

INGREDIENTS

2¼ cups Granulated Sugar
⅔ cup Water
Pinch of Cream Of Tartar
½ cup Butter
1t. Vinegar
⅔ cup Heavy Cream
6 Ripe Eating Apples

METHOD

❦ Heat the sugar and water together over a gentle heat until the sugar has dissolved. Add the cream of tartar, butter, vinegar, and cream and increase the heat so that the mixture comes to a boil.

❦ Once boiling, stir the contents of the pan continuously and heat until the temperature reaches 290°F. If you do not have a sugar thermometer you can test the syrup by dropping small amounts into cold water; on contact it should form hard threads if hot enough.

❦ Spike the apples onto wooden skewers and dip them into the sugar syrup. Roll them around the pan to ensure they are well covered and leave to cool on a lightly buttered surface.

FAIRGROUND FANCIES: BARLEY SUGAR
AND TAFFY APPLES

STICKJAW

The ultimate in schoolboy taffy, stickjaw is a great fuel supplement for high-energy activists. This is based on an authentic American recipe of the period.

INGREDIENTS

3 1/2 cups Granulated Sugar
3 1/2 cups Soft Brown Sugar
1/2 cup Glucose
5 cups Water
1t. Vanilla Essence
5 cups Shredded Coconut

METHOD

❧ Gently heat the two sugars, glucose, and water in a saucepan until the sugar has fully dissolved. Increase the heat and boil the syrup until it reaches 310°F on the sugar thermometer or hard, brittle threads form if a small amount is dropped into cold water.

❧ Remove the pan from the heat and stir in the vanilla essence and shredded coconut. As the sugar cools, the mixture will become thicker and more difficult to stir.

❧ Pour the mixture onto a greased cookie sheet and allow to cool completely before cutting into chunks.

Lemonade

Homemade lemonade complements barley sugar and taffy apples perfectly. Mrs. Beeton made hers with the juice of four lemons and the rinds of two, 1 cup sugar and 4 1/2 cups boiling water. The sugar and lemon rind were pounded together, then the strained lemon juice and boiling water added. When the sugar had dissolved, the lemonade was strained and cooled. Mrs. Beeton observed that it would be "much improved by having the white of an egg beaten up in it."

BARLEY SUGAR

Twists of barley sugar call to mind the old-fashioned merry-go-rounds with their beautifully decorated horses riding on golden, spiraling poles. Recapture a little fairground nostalgia with this recipe, based on one from Mrs. Beeton.

INGREDIENTS

3 1/2 cups Granulated Sugar
Rind and Juice of 1 Lemon
Pinch of Cream of Tartar
2 1/2 cups Water

COOK'S TIP

It is important that the sugar does not burn; the finished candies should be the color of straw.

METHOD

❧ Place the sugar and water in a saucepan and place over a low heat until the sugar has completely dissolved. Add the lemon rind and cream of tartar and bring the liquid to a boil. Continue boiling until the liquid reaches 240°F then carefully remove the lemon rind.

❧ Add the strained lemon juice to the pan and continue boiling until the temperature reaches 310°F. Remove the pan from the heat and pour the sugar onto a well-greased cookie sheet. It will begin to set as it cools.

❧ Using a sharp knife cut the barley sugar into strips, and when sufficiently cool to handle twist the strips into braids.

ORIGINAL BARLEY SUGAR
Originally, barley sugar was made by soaking barley in water overnight, then straining off the water and combining it with sugar syrup.

ACID DROPS

The *sweet and sour tang of acid drops cuts through the years to transport you back to childhood, when a fistful of acid drops or bull's eyes were the currency of the playground. This recipe is an authentic Victorian one.*

INGREDIENTS

2¼ cups Granulated Sugar
2½ cups Water
1 T. Vinegar
½ t. Tartaric Acid
1 t. Lemon Flavoring

METHOD

❧ Place the sugar, water, and vinegar in a saucepan and place over a gentle heat, stirring all the time until the sugar has dissolved.

❧ Increase the heat and bring the syrup to a fast boil, continue heating until the temperature of the syrup reaches 300°F on the sugar thermometer or forms brittle threads when small quantities of the syrup are dropped into cold water.

❧ Remove the pan from the heat and stir in the tartaric acid and lemon flavoring. Beat well, and when nearly cold break off small amounts of the mixture and form into drop shapes with your hands. Leave to set hard.

Ginger Beer

No childhood feast would have been complete
without Ginger Beer. Mrs. Beeton's recipe, which made
48 bottles, called for the juice and rind of two lemons,
1½oz fresh ginger, 1oz cream of tartar, 2 ½lb sugar,
12pt boiling water and ½oz fresh yeast. All the ingredients
except the yeast were mixed in a large pot. The yeast, creamed
with a little warm water, was added when the mixture
had cooled. The pot was left to stand overnight, covered, then
the yeasty foam skimmed off and the liquid poured into another
pot to allow the sediment to settle. Then the ginger beer
was bottled and was ready to drink after 3 days.

LEMON DROPS

These delicious candies are a treat for all children, who could help
to make them at the ball-rolling stage. A pyramid
of lemon and orange drops would make a
colorful addition to a birthday party.

COOK'S TIP

Make Orange
Drops using orange
juice and rind and
candied orange
peel.

INGREDIENTS

2¼ cups Granulated Sugar
⅔ cup Water
Grated Rind and juice of 1 Lemon
1 Egg White, Stiffly Beaten
Finely Chopped Candied Lemon Peel for Decoration

METHOD

❧ Gently heat together the sugar and water until the sugar has
dissolved completely. Increase the heat and bring the syrup to a boil,
continue boiling until the temperature reaches 240°F if using a sugar
thermometer or until a small amount of syrup dropped into cold water
forms a soft ball.

❧ Remove the pan from the heat and stir in the lemon juice and rind.
Gradually pour the syrup onto the stiffly beaten egg white, beating all
the time until the mixture is firm enough to form into small balls.

❧ Roll each ball in chopped candied lemon peel and allow to cool
completely.

BULL'S EYES

Bull's Eyes and schoolboys go together like peaches and cream.
William Brown, Richmal Crompton's incomparable hero, was a
connoisseur of these delicious sticky candies.

INGREDIENTS

4½ cups Granulated Sugar
1¼ cups Water
Pinch of Cream of Tartar
¼ t. Tartaric Acid
Few Drops of Yellow Coloring
½t. Lemon Flavoring

METHOD

❧ Place the sugar, water, and cream of tartar in a saucepan over a
gentle heat until the sugar dissolves. Increase the heat and allow the
syrup to boil to a temperature of 310°F. To achieve this accurately use
a sugar thermometer.

❧ Remove the pan from the heat and pour the syrup onto a well-
greased surface and allow to cool a little. To prevent the syrup from
spreading too much, use a greased knife to turn the edges of the
cooling taffy into the middle.

❧ When the mixture is cool enough to handle, cut a small piece and
stretch it between greased hands until it is very thin. Double the taffy
up and repeat the process until the mixture is creamy white in color.

❧ Add the tartaric acid, coloring, and lemon flavoring to the
remaining mixture and combine well. Draw the pulled sugar out into
lengths and lay them roughly 1in. apart on top of the colored portion.
Fold over the colored taffy to enclose the strips.
Pull the mixture, as above, into convenient
sizes and cut into small pieces using
buttered scissors.

*They
were forbidden
however to go anywhere
except on the down and into
the woods, the village being
especially prohibited, where huge
bull's eyes and unctuous toffy
might be procured in exchange for
coin of the realm.*

THOMAS HUGHES,
TOM BROWN'S
SCHOOLDAYS

COOK'S TIP

Eliza Actons commented that "the sugar strands will not adhere to the drops once they become hard," so decorate them when they are still warm enough. She recommends that you gently shake the drops in a bag containing the sugar strands.

BUTTERSCOTH AND CHOCOLOTE DROPS, SIMPLE WHOLESOME TREATS STRAIGHT FROM THE KITCHEN

CHOCOLATE DROPS

These delicious drops are based on a recipe from Eliza Acton. Children could have fun making them, for themselves once the heating of the chocolate has been done by an adult. For fun, you could decorate half the quantity with white or multicolored sugar strands and leave the rest plain.

INGREDIENTS

8oz Good Quality Cooking Chocolate
1 cup Confectionery Sugar, Sieved
Sugar Strands For Decoration (Optional)

METHOD

❧ Heat a small saucepan over a high heat until well warmed. Remove the pan from the heat, break the chocolate into it and pound with a wooden spoon until the chocolate is melted but still very thick.
❧ Add the sieved confectionery sugar to the pan and beat together until the two are well blended.
❧ Take small amounts of the mixture and roll quickly into small balls, Stand them on wax paper until cold. Roll the chocolate drops in sugar strands to decorate if desired.

BUTTERSCOTCH

There are many recipes for Butterscotch, a simple, wholesome candy approved of by Mrs. Beeton. This is based on her recipe.

INGREDIENTS

1¼ cups Fresh Milk
2¼ cups Granulated Sugar
1 cup Butter
Pinch of Cream of Tartar

METHOD

❧ Put the milk and sugar in a saucepan and place over a low heat until the sugar has completely dissolved. Cut the butter into small dice and add to the pan along with the cream of tartar.
❧ Increase the heat and bring the pan to a boil. Continue heating until the syrup registers 250°F on a sugar thermometer, or a small amount dropped into cold water forms a firm ball.
❧ Pour the butterscotch into a greased pan and when firm enough mark out portions using a sharp knife. Allow to cool completely before cutting into sections and wrapping in wax paper.

COOK'S TIP

To vary your butterscotch, make it with brown sugar and flavor with lemon essence.

STRAWBERRY SHERBET

This is a gorgeous pink Victorian froth, just the thing to refresh young persons who have eaten too many marshmallows. Crush 3 cups strawberries, add 7 cups water, the juice of 1 lemon and a few drops of orangeflower water. Let it stand for four hours. Put 2 cups granulated sugar in another bowl, stretch some cheesecloth over it and pour the strawberry juice through it, pushing the pulp through. Stir until the sugar is dissolved, strain again, and chill for an hour before serving.

PINK AND PRETTY MARSHMALLOWS

COOK'S TIP
Chop up marshmallows to use as a garnish or mix in with homemade ice cream.

MARSHMALLOWS

Soft, fluffy marshmallows, sweet and sticky, can be eaten on their own, or toasted by a roaring fire. This is based on Mrs. Beeton's recipe.

COOK'S TIP

To make Chocolate Marshmallows, wait until the marshmallows are completely cold, then dip them in melted chocolate.

INGREDIENTS

4oz Gum Arabic
1¼ cups Water
2 cups Confectionery Sugar
3 Egg Whites
Flavoring of Your Choice
Coloring to Match Flavoring

METHOD

❦ Place the gum arabic in a saucepan and pour in the water. Leave to soak until soft. Place the saucepan on a gentle heat and allow the gum arabic to dissolve completely before pouring the mixture through a piece of cheesecloth.

❦ Put the strained liquid back into a clean saucepan with the confectionery sugar and heat gently until the sugar dissolves, then remove the pan from the heat.

❦ Add the egg whites and whisk until the mixture is stiff then add any flavoring and coloring you like. Pour into a deep, nonstick pan. Leave to set for approximately 10 hours. When ready, cut the marshmallow into small squares and dredge with plenty of confectionery sugar.

INDEX

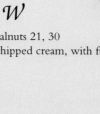